EXCERPTS FROM A

Diary

of a

Catholic Woman

Liz McGilvray

ISBN 978-1-68517-559-7 (paperback)
ISBN 978-1-68517-560-3 (digital)

Christian Faith Publishing
832 Park Avenue
Meadville, PA 16335
www.christianfaithpublishing.com

Printed in the United States of America

Whenever I know someone is in trouble, I learned to never pry but let them know I am here if they need me. What do I see when I look at you? I see beauty. Yes. I am a sinner, and I do wrong, but I always try to do better.

I call everyone *sweetheart*. Why do I do this? Because my Creator made us all. He knew us before we were a gleam in our father's and mother's eyes. I was the last of nine children, the first preemie to survive on record at six months in a Detroit hospital.

I was born during World War II, the youngest of nine. Two of my brothers at the time were stationed overseas. My father served in World War I in France; he received a bullet close to his heart. They could never take it out. He died at sixty-seven with the bullet still there. My father only had to look at you to know you will not do that again. As I grew, I saw the beautiful man he was, a softy. I would see him on his knees, praying at 4:00 a.m. and 8:00 p.m. every day. If my dad was making chop suey on Sunday, no matter if my mom changed the mealtime, all my siblings seemed to appear, but they always had somewhere to be, so as the youngest child still at home, I had to do the dishes myself.

My beautiful mother believed in helping anyone in trouble, whether it was food, money, or her last pair of nylons. My mother was always there, holding our heads over the toilet with a wet washcloth when we were sick. I told my mother I wanted to marry a poor man, just like Dad. She laughed and said we were just average. I never felt poor, just average. One of the things I admired about my mom was when anyone came home, complaining about their mates, she would say, "It's all your fault, I raised you, and I know you." She always called their spouses, sons or daughters.

I did not appreciate my older brothers and sisters until I was older. They came to visit a lot with their spouses and kids. I learned to love each one as I grew. There was only a five-year age difference between the oldest grandchild and me. I was able to see each one of them when they came home from the hospital. Fifty-eight grandchildren, including my own.

I love every niece and nephew as if they were my own children. My siblings were always there for me. In each of them, I see my dad and mom. All of them giving and not a selfish one in the bunch. Whenever I needed help or advice in anything, I was never afraid to ask any of them. Coming from a family of nine, we are all different. We came from the same parents, so we can relate to one another's views. We may not always agree but always with respect of our own beliefs and individuality.

My sisters were unexpected gifts for me, delivered by my parents, once I was old enough to realize it. I could be so mad at different situations, visit my sisters, vent there, and end up laughing before leaving. The conversation never left our free therapy sessions. I was surrounded by unconditional love and support.

At fifteen, I started to pray to the Blessed Mother for a good husband. I met my honey just before my eighteenth birthday on a blind date. I married him at twenty years old. There was not a subject that we did not talk about, even adoption, not knowing this would come to be. I was from a large Catholic family of nine. He was from a small Protestant family of three. He did learn to make the sign of the cross by creating a little jingle: "Forehead, navel, left shoulder, right." I saw him perform this under a friend's Christmas tree, intoxicated, singing the words merrily.

From youth, I wanted a home and family of my own. In my era, when a girl came home pregnant, this was a shameful experience. The shame was always upon the woman as she carried the baby. Frustrated by the injustice, I would get so upset and vowed to wait, knowing there was no man worth the suffering and shame. I never wanted a man to say to me, "I had to marry you." For me, you get the whole package or nothing at all. God comes first.

There's always temptation. I used to carry a cross in my bra. When it pricked me, it reminded me of my vow to wait, a reminder that I was worthy of giving myself to only one man, the man I would marry. I did make it to the altar by the grace of God, thanking God for giving me the strength to wait. It was extremely hard to maintain my virtue. When you love a man very much, you want all of him too.

Sadly, my dear father passed away six months before I was married. Thankfully, he was able to meet my mate before he died. After my father passed, I did not want my father, even though deceased, to be ashamed of me.

Why do we have stop signs? To protect.

We have a choice; we can stop. If we don't, we can hurt, maim, or kill others or ourselves.

What are the commandments? They are guidelines for us. When we go against them, we hurt inside. They are guidelines to protect us. We have the same choice because God gave us all free will.

When my honey and I were married, it was a mixed-faith marriage. He took instructions to know what my religion was about and agreed to sign the paper to raise our future children Catholic. Before we wed, he was at my door every Sunday at 7:30 a.m. to go to mass with me. The day after our wedding, my family met to all go to church together and lay my wedding bouquet on my father's grave.

The very next Sunday, upon waking my honey, he said, "I tried your religion, and I don't feel it holds anything for me." I am happy he did not convert to Catholicism as I would have hated him for not practicing it. I do, however, greatly admire my husband as he made sure the children attended mass and catechism. He was also there for each of their sacraments.

As newlyweds, my husband and I were unable to conceive a baby of our own. Happily, we fostered many babies. They brought us so much joy. Just when they were starting to get their little personalities, smiles, and coos, they would go back to their mothers or be adopted out. A sadness would come over me, but then they would place another gift for us to love and spoil and bring so much joy.

After four years of marriage and still no children, I felt sad. I wanted children of our own so desperately. A special foster boy came and stayed with us for over nine months. The agency called and told us he was going to be adopted. What a nightmare! His smile could brighten up a room. I stormed heaven and our heavenly Mother with prayers for this little boy. By the grace of God, he became ours. I had applied for another boy, and during the adoption process, a little girl became available. So precious was she. These children stole our hearts. Afterward, the adoption agency told us we could not adopt anymore as there was a shortage. I wanted more. These precious souls are only on loan to us to teach and do our best as they belong to our Creator.

After ten years of marriage and spiking my husband's morning coffee with Lourdes holy water, I became pregnant. I could not believe it, and five more healthy children soon followed. Yes, a total of seven wonderful gifts. Thank you, God. Every time a child came into our home, I loved my honey more.

He said, "I don't care if you have zero or if you have twelve." Thank you, God, for sending this man my way. He would always sing, "If I was single again, my pockets would jingle again." Did we fight? Absolutely, just never in front of our children.

I was consumed with worry of how we would make it. Just when the worry would become overwhelming, another special life bloomed in me, and it would take my mind off the worry. My last child was born just before my forty-third birthday. After her birth, I had to go back to work. I constantly prayed, "Please, Lord, watch over her." I had been one of the lucky ones to be able to stay home and raise my children.

Could I afford the first? No. Could I afford the last? No. I don't have many worldly goods. However, one daughter once told me, "Mom, don't you know you already won the lotto? You have a loving, close family."

Now I know why my parents had nine. It was easy when the children were little. They are heavy on your lap. When they're older, they become heavy on your heart. Thank you, God, for the wonderful journey. It's been quite a ride. I did not have the time to get bored. I cannot begin to tell you all the miracles I have had in fifty-seven and a half years of marriage.

When we got married, we promised one another to always do what we thought was right, and hindsight is great. When we had children, we learned to never leave our children alone in our home. One of us was always there. Also, never let our children babysit their siblings as you would have thought Hitler had now taken over. We had three key rules for the home.

One—Mass on Sunday. In my day, everyone went to church on Sundays. That is what you did. Stores were closed on Sunday.

Two—No drugs. If you did this, you don't live here, and believe me, it came to pass when our sixteen-year-old had to be told to leave. He could not come home until he got help. He did come home util he was eighteen, and drugs were found again, and he had to leave again and live on his own. He has turned out to be a beautiful man. Thank you, God.

Three—No locked doors in our home as that tells us you are hiding something. I came across an X-rated video in my home. Who would bring this garbage into our home? I ripped the tape apart and left a note on the table, saying, "Don't bring this garbage into our home." It never happened again to my knowledge.

I have never said, "My child would never do this." With seven kids, there was a good chance they did do it, and it had probably been going on for a while! Looking back, I thank my parents for instilling my deep faith and trust in God, but most of all by teaching through example and not preaching.

Being pregnant, I had asthma where sometimes I coughed all the time, 24-7. One time in particular, the doctor treating me did not want to give me an x-ray as I was pregnant. The doctor sent me to an unfamiliar neighborhood for a special x-ray, and my lovely sister was with me. We became so disoriented that we ended up going down a one-way street, the wrong way! Would you believe no one beeped their horn? They were as shocked as we were.

My grocery budget each week was twenty dollars. My sister had called and asked if I could come and cut her boy's hair. I said I would be over after I finished grocery shopping. On the way to my sister, I said to God, "Well, I spent my grocery allowance, and I don't have any meat for the week."

As I entered my sister's house, her husband had just come in from hunting. "You must take meat home. My freezer is full," my sister said. I declined and was grateful as we did not eat venison. She said, "No, it is beef. It will go to waste as we must make room in the freezer for the venison." Prayers—always answered when most needed. Thank you, God.

When my honey was laid off from work, brothers and sisters would leave groceries on the porch. God bless these special loving people. I would never tell them I needed it. They were just there. We fell on tough times and eventually did lose our home. I was lucky, up to that point, to be able to stay home with our children. No one has such devotion and willing investment as parents do to their children. Our last child was born just before my forty-third birthday, and I had to go back to work. It was so hard to leave her to go to work. I constantly prayed as she was only nine months, "Please, God, watch over her."

We had a beautiful neighbor who, every Easter and Christmas, would send a big ham for Easter and a turkey for Thanksgiving. One time, my honey was out of work. The eighties were tough to find employment. I had been in the bedroom, praying to God to help us out of this vicious circle. We just could not find our way out. I had one big turkey and nothing else to make the Thanksgiving meal. Talk about a special delivery!

As I left the bedroom, there was a knock on my door, and a man and a lady that I had never met before handed me an envelope with money in it. They said they knew we were having a rough time. I asked, "Who can I send a thank you note to?"

They told me God had sent them.

I went into the bathroom, laid prostrate on the floor, and could not stop crying. Thank you, God.

In my home, every time a new life was born, it was a celebration to us all. That is why I love new life so much. Newborns are pure, no hate, no resentment, no unhealthy habits, the look of an angel who just left heaven to give me a new purpose in life and to take away my own selfishness. God sent me these gifts, but now at seventy-nine, believe me, they are my gifts now.

I could be very stern with the children while showing them what I thought was right. I tried anyway, but when they got sick, I was done a sobbing mess. My honey was the softy. They would ask him first knowing they might get a yes. We learned to check with one another to see what the other one said as children are smart. If one parent gave the punishment, it was up to that parent to lift it.

I did not allow our children to stay overnight anywhere. I wanted to know they were safe at home. I cannot go to your home and ask what kind of morals you have. You would have thrown me off the porch. I did not want my children in a vulnerable situation. So as a mom, I was known as the green mean machine who never allowed sleepovers.

When you have a child in trouble, you just do not know what to do or where to go for help. Children don't come with instructions. I had dark days when I thought, *Will they survive?*

When you have a child on drugs. When you think you will lose one of them. How will I pay this bill? How are we going to make it financially? I have felt every emotion I know raising my children.

I have always been a tough love parent. You made the mistakes; you take the consequences. I had a child in trouble and searched for help. I called social services. They asked if I beat her. I said no. "Sorry, we cannot help you."

I called the court system. "Can you help me with this child?"

They told me no, they were the aftereffect.

Desperate, I went to the local police station and explained to him that she hates us, does not want to live here, does not follow our rules, and has no respect for her parents.

He said, "That's easy. We can sign an incorrigibility paper, and that will put her through the court system."

We put her into the court system before she got there herself. She had to answer to the courts. Thank you, God, for sending the beautiful people our way to put our daughter on the right path. She grew into a beautiful woman who is married with three daughters of her own and now works with people with mental health issues.

Today, it is hard to teach children morals. The outside world says we are free, that we have a right to do what we want. The outside world forgets to mention, however, that there is always a price to pay, and sometimes a high price that lasts a lifetime. I would do about anything to keep my children safe.

Talking to our boys, telling them to remember, "A woman is not just a piece of meat to be used." I thought I was just worried about my daughters, but you are worried about your boys too. For one minute of pleasure, it could be a life of misery.

I had a child come home from school and tell me that I must go to the principal's office in the morning or he could not go back to school. I refused to go to the principal. The principal called me the next morning and asked, "Did he not tell you that you had to come today?"

I stated that, yes, he had told me. I told him that my son had done the wrong. Whatever he did, he would have to make it right. I never received another call from the principal's office.

My sixteen-year-old son thought he was ingenious, sneaking his girlfriend through the bedroom window at 2:00 a.m., not realizing sounds travel to our bedroom right above his. I love those type of surprises. You feel like a real SWAT team busting in that door!

9

A family moved in next door, no father in the home, and the mother worked nights. She had five beautiful daughters, and I had two teen roosters in the house. A nightmare.

One night, my two boys were in bed when I went to bed. At 2:00 a.m., my phone rang. My honey worked nights, so I thought he was in trouble. When I answered, no one was there. I decided to go back to bed, and again, the phone rang. I went to check the time in my son's bedroom to find he was not there. I ran downstairs. My other son was missing as well. Oh no, the roosters got loose!

I headed next door in my big boots and fuzzy robe and knocked on the family of five beautiful daughters' door. I could see through a small octagon window one of my boys was cleaning up dog feces. After banging the door down, someone finally answered the door. I told him, "Get home, and where is your brother?"

Famous saying: "I don't know."

My voice was very loud. "Get home, and I am not leaving without your brother."

The oldest of the girls peeked her head down the stairs to tell me that he had just jumped out the second-story window, not hurt. Thank you, God. Maybe that is why he became a paratrooper in the army. He had experience.

My first child was my greatest teacher. As he is throwing a huge temper tantrum, he tells me that if I give him what he wants, he will stop this tantrum. Thank you, God, for this early lesson. It was going to be over my dead body.

Another child would throw temper tantrums so bad when he was told no he would turn blue. At first, I thought he had a brain tumor. What is wrong with him? I learned to pick him up and put him on the bedroom floor and tell him, "When you have a smile, you can come out." Some of the children's temper tantrums created plenty of holes in the wall. They know how to fill holes; they have had plenty of experience.

I first experienced this while watching my nephew. I had never experienced a child turning blue. I cannot tell you how scary that was. I told my sister, "You should hang him from the chandelier by his collar."

Ironically, I had a child that did the same thing. Her response was, "Do you want me to send over that chandelier?"

Kids say the funniest things. Here are a few I can remember.

"When I grow up, I am going to marry Dad."

Telling a little one that we were going to have a baby, he said, "You better tell Dad as I can't drive you to the hospital."

"Why does Dad have to be a prostitute and not Catholic?" She meant to say Protestant.

"Why do I have to go to church and Dad does not?"

"Because he is not Catholic."

"Well, if you ask me, there are too many Catholics in the car. Now can I just go home with Dad?"

"What do you think your mom is going to have, a boy or girl?"

"Whatever God wants."

"I wanted you to have another baby, so I threw coins down the sewer drain."

My children went through the neighborhood with a red wagon, selling jewelry their grandmother had given to them. They were going to help the poor people down the street but really were hitting the candy store.

A child came home from kindergarten, telling me this dog followed him home. The only problem was the dog had a rope around his neck.

A child going after school to the JCPenney department store, running the elevator and accepting money for doing so. No, he does not work there.

"Dad, what are you waiting for?"

"A train."

"Can I wait with you?"

No train tracks, just standing in the backyard.

Dad getting his coat on. "Dad, where are you going?"

"Crazy."

"Can I come?"

One daughter getting ready for school, coming down the stairs with her coat and snow pants on. I didn't know at the time, but she was wearing my wedding dress underneath. She wanted to look beautiful for the dance at school. She wanted a dress that would twirl. This dress is willed to her.

A famous saying in our house was, "When we win the lotto." This was said to the children when they wanted something we could not afford. "When I win the lotto and get rich, I will buy you anything you want."

I love these children with my whole being. The outside world does not. Because you are different, I don't love you less. I may not agree with you. If you are not married and want to sleep in our home in the same room, not happening. Do I respect you? Yes, I do. Do I love you less? No, I just do not agree with you. If you want to have a same-sex bedroom in our home, not happening. Do I respect you? Yes. Do I love you less? No. I just do not agree with you.

I have the United Nations in our home: French, German, Polish, Scottish, Irish, Hispanic, Arabic and African American. Do I respect you? Yes. Do I love you less? No. Do I love each one of you?

Yes. I have many religions in my home. Do I respect your faith? Yes. Do I love you less? No.

Catholics are not the only ones in heaven. My faith has brought comfort. I do not know how one can survive without it. Thank you, Dad and Mom. Please keep me safe, God. I know you are but a whisper away.

Every baby deserves the right to have a mother and a father. Our children knew how I felt, so when I heard my unwed daughter was pregnant, she wanted to know if I was happy for her. "No," I said. "You have a long and tough road ahead of you. This is what you wanted, now you go live with it."

I am not raising grandchildren. I still have children at home to raise. I could never agree to put my daughters on the pill as this was me saying that this is okay for sexual intimacy before marriage. Do I love you less? No. I hurt for you. I want your mate to love, respect, and care for you and have self-control. I want you to be able to give one another confidence, and above all, love God first. Hindsight is great. Did I do right? And, yes, I am a sinner. I thank God for my honey. When he looks at me, he still warms my heart. Do we fight? Yes, just never in front of the children.

We learned through our mistakes. Sometimes it takes a two-by-four to hit us over our heads. I hope the laws of marriage stay the same as God has intended. If you want to live differently, don't call it marriage. You can have a paper stating that you are partners. Do I respect you? Yes. Do I love you less? No. I do not agree with you. However, I am not your judge. God is in charge. What I hope for our family and the beautiful people who have entered our lives is that they know:

God is just a whisper away.

Ask God to be of service to help when and where needed.

Know what to say to console anyone hurting.

God gave me free will, let me use it wisely.

God, please hold me in the palm of your hand.

I remember when the people had to vote on Roe v. Wade. They voted it down. A girl who is underaged can go into an abortion clinic, have an abortion, and not let her parent know. The saying is, "It's their body, they have a right to do so." The law states that parents are responsible until their children are eighteen years of age. There is always a bully on the block if you allow it.

I hear many that say this war is because of God. War is greed, selfishness, and killing, one wanting something you have no right to. Killing people because they do not agree with your identity or belief is tragic.

I can still see the woman's face who was offended to hear prayer in public. To take the Ten Commandments out of sight, how sad. They are guidelines. What are you so afraid of?

We deserve the freedom of respect from one another. God says love one another. He is not asking us to kill, maim, belittle, call names, or make someone uncomfortable, one thinking they are king of the mountain and *You must think like I do, or I can have you beheaded as I am better than you.*

We are all humans who make mistakes. God is for all religions. Love one another. As one daughter said to me, "God does not make junk." We all have free will to choose what we want. Why do so many want to come to America? For the life of freedom and the pursuit of happiness. My hope for America is the strength to stand for what is right, not for what I can line my pockets with.

My honey and I were both from Detroit and met on a blind date. Every time the car factories went down, it would affect my honey's job. We were losing our home, my oldest child was getting married, and we had six more to still care for.

At first, it was devasting, then it became survival. That is all that mattered. I called my older brother in Florida and asked him what our chances would be there. He told me it was not good. I thought at one point if I must live in a tent, it would be easier to clean but a no go.

One of my neighbors met and married a beautiful man from northern Michigan. She invited the family up north for haying season. My honey and the older kids went. I stayed home with the younger ones. She called and said, "I know your family can make it up here." My honey and kids had a ball, working hard, and eating good. Remember, we are city folk.

She told the neighbors that we were relatives and coming to live up here. So her husband's father was kind enough to take my honey around looking for work. If you asked how far it is, not far, about ten miles down the road.

Later, the car broke down. The story is, I must send away for a part. It will be in about a week. It was our only car.

Boy, I miss the city. I miss all the family that was my support. I live here, but downstate is my home. I have been up here for twenty-eight years and, going home, I now wonder, *How do they ever drive in all that traffic?*

We have lived in five houses since we have been married, and these are my experiences along the way. Our first home in Detroit had two bedrooms, one bathroom, and a finished upstairs. It had a huge backyard with a long rolling hill that the children would slide down in the wintertime on cookie sheet pans. Our firstborn liked to take his clothes off on the hill. Embarrassing!

Next to the house, there was an easement with a gas station where my husband worked. If I needed to talk to him, we had a long enough hose to stretch from our home to the gas station. He would see me waving my hands in the air, which was the signal. We would each pick up the hose and talk through it. It beat yelling.

We lived in a great neighborhood. The family next door had three older sons. The first one was graduating high school when we moved in. The mom of those three boys was over most days to hug all the foster babies. Her husband loved to take pictures of our kids. I'm happy for that as I would never have had any otherwise.

Our water went out, and I did not want to call the plumber because it was the weekend, so our neighbor connected his outdoor hose and ran it to my kitchen window so I could have water. We always spent the Fourth of July at their house. He would buy the pepperoni, and I would make it into pepperoni rolls. Her mother would make tarts that were so delicious. We would watch fireworks at the end of the night.

Our neighbors became our first son's godparents. She loved flowers and would be in the backyard often. One of our daughters at nine months got extremely sick. It was thought we were going to lose her. She was in the children's hospital downtown, which was a long way from our home. You could only be there at specific times. I cried a lot.

My son told his godmother, "Mom doesn't love me anymore." When you have a sick or troubled child, it's hard to think of anything else. Now I know what God means when he said you leave the ninety-nine sheep and try to find the lost one. During this time, someone left twenty dollars in my cupboard so I could visit my daughter two more times. It only took me twenty years to find out that my sister put it there. Thank you, God.

In our neighborhood, there was a gentleman who asked if he could give the children gum. Every time he walked by, he would throw them each a piece of gum. The children were so excited. They would say, "Here comes the gum man."

When they were waiting on the lawn for the gum man, we had a big tree close to the easement near the gas station that the kids could play for hours in a huge sandpit with their cars, trucks, and toys. They would dig so much my honey had to fill that hole a couple of times, but it was nice to know they were safe and enjoying themselves.

Another wonderful lady I met at our church had a beautiful family. I will never forget her. Her daughter was babysitting just down the street for another family on New Year's Eve. The mother spoke with her daughter at midnight to say, "Happy New Year!" That would be their last conversation. Her sixteen-year-old daughter was abducted from the home and killed by a neighborhood boy.

We lived in Detroit, but across the street was Redford Township. The bussing system had changed and wanted to bus the children twenty-eight miles to the inner city for school. We did not make much money and could not afford the Catholic school tuition. I knew what money was coming in and what monies were going out.

I talked to the nuns to see if I could work in the school in the late afternoons, into the evenings. As soon as my honey came in the door for work, I was going out. Our children were able to attend a safe school and walk to and from school by themselves. Thank you, God. They were kind enough to give us this opportunity.

Our second home was to be our dream home. It was spacious, and we were right across the street from the school park where my husband attended elementary school. We played a lot of kickball and tag in that field. We tried to renovate the house to fit us all, plus my husband's parents. Sadly, the large houses have large bills, and when my husband lost his job, we lost our house. The dream became a nightmare.

My husband owned his own landscaping company. While one of my daughters was working with him, she saw a beautiful bird, and she asked her dad if she caught it, could she keep it? He said, "Yes."

Guess what? She caught it. He then had to break her heart as she could not keep it. She was so crushed. Be careful what you say if when you think it is impossible, it is possible. This same daughter grew her own wings and flew beyond our dream to the Philippines as an exchange student for a year.

On one occasion, my kindergarten son was told to go to the office. He was too afraid, so he left the school, crossed a busy street, and walked over a half a mile home. I was at the pediatric office with a sick child and had no idea. The principal ended up chasing this kindergartener through the field across from our house once his absence was discovered. I would have loved to see the video from this.

I used to have a triangle bell that hung from a tree in the backyard. This was used as my signal for the children to come home for mealtimes or nightly curfew. I could see them coming from all different directions.

There was a family that lived just around the block from us. My son used to like to go and play with their little boy. He had asked to stay the night. Of course, that was out of the question. A few weeks later, the husband had killed that little boy, five, his wife, and himself. His daughter was shot at but survived. I always wondered why. This was a tragedy.

I discovered two of my daughters were smoking with a cigarette found in my purse. "Well," I asked, "do you want to learn how to smoke?"

They said, "Yes."

I stated, "You can't waste cigarettes, so I will show you how."

As we started our smoking lesson, there was a knock at the door, and a child at the door wanted to know if the girls could come out and play.

"No," was her reply, "we are smoking with our mom."

I lit it for them and told them, "You inhale like this." Well, it didn't take long, and they did get sick. They never took cigarettes again.

When moving north, we ended up in a cabin. That was all we could find. If you have ever seen *Tobacco Road*, this was it. My honey wondered what he did to his family when pulling up to this cabin. This cabin had one living room that held two sets of bunk beds for the four girls, one bedroom for me and my honey, and a small kitchen with a window that opened into a sun porch. Yep, another set of bunk beds on the sunporch for the two boys.

I could wash dishes and watch the boys sleep at the same time. The kitchen was so small I could cook the meals and turn around and serve at the same time. It was small but held some of the funniest new experiences for these city folk. The cabin couldn't hold much more than bedding, clothes, and food. We were grateful for the indoor plumbing. Thank you, God.

We rented the cabin from Grandma and Grandpa B. Grandma B made the best cookies and was sure to send them over. We were surrounded by dirt roads and woods. There was a swimming pond just down the road at a golf-type resort that had residential homes. My youngest daughter almost drowned in that pond. I have never learned to swim, so this was a reoccurring nightmare I had. We were surrounded by water in Northern Michigan. Lakes, ponds, and rivers were everywhere. As city folk, we had much to learn.

The next house we rented was a big farmhouse. It was down the road from our previous neighbor from near Detroit. It had a huge living room that held two couches, two chairs, a bookcase, and a TV, plenty of room to walk around with one big front window and a side window. The dining room had a window with a woodstove for heat. The kitchen had lots of cupboards with a stackable washer and dryer. There was also a bedroom and bathroom on the main floor. Upstairs had three bedrooms. We now had plenty of space and new experiences to enjoy.

Our bedroom on the main floor had a drop ceiling. At night, I could hear the mice running on the ceiling. I had the hardest time to sleep as my fear of mice falling on my head while I slept was a continuing nightmare. The windows were old and rattled. All our food was kept in airtight containers or glass jars. I was not sharing our food with the local mice. One of the boys wanted to be captain of the mousetraps until he had to empty the traps. The captain jumped ship.

We knew if the lights flickered, we had to run the water. The well had an electric pump, so we would have no water. It was all hands on deck, start filling. One night, when I woke, I swore I heard water running. I thought one of the kids left the water running in the bathroom. As my feet hit the floor, I was in water. The water line had broken behind the toilet. My honey woke to one big flood. The water shutoff was down a long driveway to the other side of the fence that backed up to the telephone pole to shut it off. Did I forget to mention? It was waist-deep snow as well.

Living up on the hill, we were isolated, and of course, we had four young hens in the house. Many boys came by. They were a great bunch. There was always snowball fights, tag, and just clean fun. We had no TV signal, so they would bring movies to watch.

Our septic system never seemed to drain properly. There was always a bad spot by the side of the house. The kids never mentioned this to new visitors. Their friends quickly learned where it was located, and we knew by the way they smelled afterward. Not always clean fun, but fun nonetheless. Their only activity was roller-skating on Saturdays and church on Sundays.

Of course, the washing machine had broken, and to find a secondhand one was tough. We did eventually find a wringer washer; we could not bring this in the house we rented as it leaked oil. We put this outside by the water spicket. Northern Michigan in March is cold. There I was, in my rubber gloves up to my elbows, doing the laundry for eight people outside. My greatest thrill was hanging the clothes out on the line and watching the wind carry them back and forth.

During one of these times, my four-year-old daughter and the dog disappeared. Panic set in. The saying trying to find a needle in a haystack ran through my mind. I decided to get to the neighbors. By neighbors, I mean at least one-fourth of a mile away. I heard giggling, her and the dog hiding behind a building. I did not know if I should spank her or hug her.

This was the year of the tent worms. So gross. They were all over everything—the house, the car, the roads. Have you ever seen the roads bleed green? I used my clotheslines as slingshots to get them off the clotheslines before I could hang the laundry to dry. What a nightmare.

Winters are long in Northern Michigan. I finally thought the winter was over. I washed all the winter clothing and prepared to put them away. When a beautiful teacher from the hill called and asked what I was doing, I was excited to tell her that I was washing and putting the winter gear away. That sweetheart asked, "Why? We will still have three more winter storms."

She was right. Have you ever seen a grown woman cry over snow? I did.

Visitors on the hill were not always human. Our neighbors' cows always appeared in our yard. One son and the dog were teasing them, and the bull got mad and started a stampede. All I could say was, "Hail Mary full of grace, run, run, run." He made it. Thank you, God.

The first time I ever saw the northern lights was on the hill. When you would drive down the hill, it was beautiful. It was like a canopy over your head, and the trees just seemed to glisten. God is here.

Knowing our only source of heat for this drafty house was wood, we dug in. My honey would come from work, cut wood, and the kids would fill the truck, and a line formed to get it in the cellar to be stacked. We were so proud as we had never done anything like this before. We were told that it was not enough wood for the long winter ahead. January, we ran out of wood. No one had wood to sell nor did we have the money to buy. One of the boys that used to visit on the hill, his father sold us some, but it was wet, so it never got warm enough.

We have four daughters, so the boys soon came to the hill. No matter how bad the snow was, they always seemed to make it up. It always snowed more on the hill than in town. The bus would pick the kids up at 6:30 a.m., and they didn't get home till 4:30 p.m. It took them one and a half hours every morning to get to school and home. One of the kids would get sick on the bus, so I stuffed his pockets with peppermints.

One of the boys got into a fight at school and had to spend the day in the same room. By the end of the day, they were friends. He had asked our son to go fishing. Our son gladly accepted. When he didn't get off the school bus, I asked the other children, "Where is your brother?"

Famous answer: "I don't know." We had just gotten a phone, and no one knew the number. On a Friday night in the fall, everyone was at the football game. I could not get a hold of anyone at the school. We were about to call the police when the young man and his father brought my son home at 7:00 p.m.

My son was running through the bleacher and knocked himself unconscious. He was taken to the hospital. I was over forty-five minutes away. I was able to get a hold of my honey at work who was able to make it to the hospital. My son's principal stayed with him until his father was able to get there. When my son returned home, he did not know us. This lasted for several hours. Thank you, God, for the safe return of my son.

The final and fifth house we moved to was in town. City folk once again. We moved into a house that needed repairs. Old lath and plaster were crumbling behind the ugly brown paneling. I learned that if you don't like something, just rip it apart. The stories I have of ripping things apart don't always go back together so easily. I found that if I started ripping the walls down in February, I could put it all out for the city's annual spring pickup. The city has most of our home, and as usual, God sent many angels our way to help us put it back together.

Parents never want to hear fighting among siblings because you love them all. On this occasion, the two boys were at it. It was bad. They had bunk beds in a small room. My honey went and chopped the beds in half and left his butt print in the drywall while moving the beds. Another hole to fix. We were unsure if the beds would ever stand on their own. They did. One bed went upstairs and one bed downstairs. I would go to one son and tell him his brother was hurting and tell the other son the same. It eventually ended. Unlike the beds, they have stayed together.

We found out one of our teenage sons was illegally helping himself to money from his work. My husband called the police on him. When the police officer arrived, the three of them went to the gentleman's store, and my son explained what he had been doing. The owner was kind enough to let him work off his debt. At the end of each night, he would offer him a cold pop. Thank you, God.

My youngest daughter had a bedroom on the second floor. I heard a noise on the roof. By the time I got there, no one was there. I knew someone was on the roof to her bedroom window. As I was going upstairs, I heard glass breaking. Two of the sunporch windows had been smashed, no doubt from the hurried exit off the roof. I didn't find out until years later it was her now husband. If I would have had my way, I would have nailed the windows shut.

Our son wanted to go into the military as soon as he graduated from high school, and he did. We became channel surfers, always watching the news to hear of anything as he was sent to Bosnia.

On Christmas Eve, my honey and I could not get him off our minds. I was washing dishes, and the phone rang. It was a stranger on the line telling us he had seen our son interviewed on TV. This man was from our hometown and called our local chamber of commerce in town to find us. The gentleman was a retired army man himself and was kind enough to send us a videotape of our son. He was okay. Thank you, God.

When my daughter was an exchange student, we did not celebrate our usual Christmas. We waited for her to come home in June. The youngest daughter received two Santa gifts. I did Christmas shopping in January and February. I got a lot for my money. The only problem is the children were not as excited to receive winter clothes in June. After she was home from the Philippines for a few days, she was found crying in her bedroom. What could be wrong? We had waited a whole year for her. She was missing the host families and all the fun she left behind.

Our youngest son would use his paycheck to buy nuts for the squirrels that would come into our yard. They would crawl all over him. He would go into town in the park and perform for the tourists. He asked me if I wanted to go and watch him. I stated, "No, I don't want to see you get rabies shots."

A Saturday in June, I decided to surprise my son-in-law for his birthday and bring him a cake in the morning. I knew they would be up by 8:00 a.m. as they have two toddlers. When I arrived, no one was awake. If you could have seen my son-in-law's face as I knocked on their bedroom window to see me standing there with a cake. He stated, "Oh, no, it's your mom."

My daughter's reply was, "It is okay, we're married."

Our oldest son was in a horrific accident at work. An explosion that engulfed him and burned 50 percent of his body. My nephew had come north, camping, and was just at our house the day previously to take showers and visit with us. I had received the call, and my son was in a downstate hospital. The daily bus had already left our town and was at time a nine-to-twelve-hour ride, depending on the route.

My niece called me and said my son was in very bad shape. Our car was old and would not make the trip downstate, so I called my nephew who was camping. He was at my home within an hour. I took our youngest daughter and whatever monies I could gather from my tips and my daughters' tips from waitressing to make the trip. My husband was left at home as he had to work and keep the other children on track. This was the longest ride of my life.

I continually prayed and begged God for him to be okay. I had to make it there to see him. Two of my sisters had made it to the hospital and put a scapular on him for me. I talked to God the entire way down, asking him to just hold him for me.

On the next weekend, my honey's boss had him go downstate to drop something off for him, which was five blocks from the hospital, a company truck and gas card to go down with. If a son ever needed his father, it was then. He was bandaged from head to foot. The only thing I could see were his eyes.

All the nurses in that burn unit were volunteers as they knew how critical the job was. The burns have to be scrubbed down, shaved, and then medication applied and wrapped every day. The pain medicine does not stop the intense pain. The patient just feels as if they are being tortured daily. You can never imagine how well God is able to work things out. Thank you, God. My son was saved.

I don't have enough thanks for all the wonderful people that have come into our lives and the blessings they bring. Our car was totaled in an accident. We again were in a situation where we were not financially able to replace the car and not certain how to move forward. We needed a car. My honey thought of calling our oldest son and borrowing money for a car. Are you kidding? We have no way to pay him back. Our children, unbeknownst to us, bought us a new car.

During that same time frame, our furnace went out in our house. At 9:00 p.m., three of my nephews left downstate and drove north, arriving at 2:00 a.m. to fix our furnace. Again, how blessed we are to be a part of a large loving family who would drop everything to help us in our times of need. Thank you, God. You have always been the solution.

I have lived a simple life. I have put God first, loved and devoted myself to only one man, raised my children to be loving, giving, and responsible. I have tried to be the best representation of my parents' sacrifices. I always look for the beauty in everyone that I meet. I have made curtains out of lace tablecloths over twenty years ago that still hang in my windows to this day. Who knew lace tablecloths and fishing line would give me such a thrill rather than a new dress? I would have rather spent money on the few luxuries I could grant my children or something for our home. I still shop at secondhand stores as many of my children do.

My wonderful marriage and seven beautiful children are my legacy. Here is a brief look of my ruffians:

My first baby, a son, who is married and the proud father of five children. One child was lost in a car accident, and the pain and void it leaves never goes away.

My second baby, a daughter, is married with one daughter and two grandsons.

My third baby, a daughter, is married with five children. Their oldest child, who had a daughter, is deceased due to a drug overdose. My daughter went on to adopt her granddaughter at the age of forty-four.

My fourth baby, a daughter, is married with three boys that keep her busy.

My fifth baby, a son, married, with one dog that minds better than any of my children ever did.

My sixth baby, a son, married with two boys and a daughter.

My seventh baby, a daughter, married with three girls.

They are all hardworking and good to their fellow humans and are assets in this world. I am still on my knees, but that is what mothers do.

Coming home from church on Sunday morning on the way to get doughnuts, I stopped at a red light. Thinking it had changed, I procced to go, and everyone followed. The problem was the light was still red. I always told the kids to be leaders, not followers. I would pray that if they drank liquor, please make them sick so they don't make it a habit. If I heard them hugging that porcelain bowl, I was celebrating. I admire the parents they have become. Grandchildren are a great bonus to life.

Our beautiful miracles all have good mates, and the grandchildren bring much joy.

I was lucky to find a good man from a loving family. I did win the lotto.

My heavenly Mother, thank you. You sent me my life partner who I prayed for, and you delivered just for me. His parents raised an incredible man and father to our children. No one understands like another mother. I don't know what is ahead of me, but here is my disclaimer to my children: if I don't know you, I love you; if I scream at you, I love you; if I am angry or ornery, I love you.

Love,

Mom

OXOXOXOXOX

About the Author

Liz is from a family of nine. She is the youngest and last living of her siblings and parents. Her brothers and sister were her best teachers. Her wonderful parents never ran out of patience with her, even though she tested them to their limits.

She lost her partner in crime over two years ago. She currently resides in Petoskey, Michigan, where she always has her kids and grandkids surrounding her with love and laughter.

CPSIA information can be obtained
at www.ICGtesting.com
Printed in the USA
BVHW042139071122
651420BV00005B/98

9 781685 175597